More praise for Ben Gaa:

"Ben Gaa has the amazing ability to find the poetry in every possible moment no matter how small or trivial. After reading his work it is impossible not to see the simple beauty in the world around us and poetic potential in all the things we tend to overlook every day. This collection of poems spans the depth and scope of his poetic ability and gives us everything we need to be inspired by the world around us."

-Bryan Rickert, author of *Fish Kite*, Editor of *The Living Senryu Anthology*

More praise for Ben Gaa:

"Having delighted us with the award-winning *Wishbones,* Ben Gaa continues to deliver exquisitely crafted haiku and senryu in *One Breath.* Gaa is a modern Midwestern *flâneur,* who is as likely to find an epiphany while drinking coffee or beer as while observing a sunset or a snowflake. Like the Japanese masters, he values the suchness of each experience, and merges humour and *karumi* with deep reflections on love and life which are wise but never didactic. His alert engagement of all five senses, combined with his expert writing and editing skills, results in work which is evocative, moving and inspirational."

-Maeve O'Sullivan, haijin and poet (*New & Selected Haiku,* forthcoming from Alba Publishing).

One Breath

Haiku & Senryu by Ben Gaa

Kansas City — Spartan Press — Missouri

Spartan Press
Kansas City, Missouri
spartanpresskc.com

Copyright © Ben Gaa, 2020
First edition: 1 3 5 7 9 10 8 6 4 2
ISBN: 978-1-952411-21-2
LCCN: 2020938053

Author photo: Jim McGowin
All rights reserved. No part of this publication may be reproduced or transmitted in any form or by any means, electronic or mechanical, including photocopying, recording or by info retrieval system, without prior written permission from the author.

This book would not be possible without the collaboration and outreach of Jason Ryberg of Spartan Press as well as poet and journalist Stefene Russell and one amazing show at CBGB's on South Grand in St. Louis, MO. Thanks also go out to the wonderful writing community here in this region, especially to those who I meet with regularly to workshop and talk shop such as John J. Han, Bryan Rickert, John Dunphy, Lori Becherer, Lisa Porter and the Mississippi Mud Dauber's Haiku Group as well as Autumn Rinaldi, Dawn Leslie Lenz, Denise Mussman, Jennifer Lynn, Lisa Ebert, Brandi Wills and the (UN)Stable Writers Group. Special thanks also goes out to the many reading series and writing institutions in my neck of the woods that have provided opportunities for me to give readings, run workshops, and network.

I would also like to send a BIG THANK YOU to the editors of the following journals, anthologies and chapbooks around the world where these poems first appeared. I've learned and continue to learn a lot from you both in the poems that you've selected of mine as well as through the ones you didn't. I also want to thank my fellow contributors to these publications. I'm continually inspired by you and your work. For those reading this book who are hungry for more great haiku and senryu, please check out these publications. You will not be disappointed:

Acorn, A Handful of Stones, A Hundred Gourds, Akitsu Quarterly, Atoms of Haiku Volume III, Blithe Spirit, Cattails, Chrysanthemum, deLuge Journal, Failed Haiku, Fiddle in the Floorboards, Fireflies' Light, Frogpond, Hedgerow, Haiku: A Concise Anthology, Heart Breaths: Book of Contemporary Haiku, Incense Dreams, Modern Haiku, Noon, OnStL, Prune Juice, Seashores, Shamrock, Sonic Boom, South by Southeast, Stardust Haiku, The Bamboo Hut, The Heron's Nest, The Mainichi Daily, The New English Verse, Tinywords, Under the Basho, Wales Haiku Journal, Wasp Shadows, and *World Haiku Review.*

-Ben Gaa

TABLE OF CONTENTS

alone again / 1

shadows lengthening / 1

agreeing to therapy / 1

corner pub / 2

catching the wrong eye / 2

twilight / 2

spring afternoon / 3

the itch / 3

still night… / 3

restless night / 4

blood moon / 4

unable to let it go / 4

pulling a pen from her hair / 5

fireworks / 5

sultry night / 5

poetry reading / 6

backyard weeds / 6

sudden storm— / 6

dew light / 7

the moth blending into / 7

midnight / 7

all day / 8

slowing down the street / 8
snow becomes / 8
garden shop / 9
election sermon / 9
empty sky / 9
rising early / 10
morning drizzle / 10
deep within the paint / 10
twilight / 11
spring moon / 11
moon viewing / 11
her promise / 12
the heat / 12
switching tempo / 12
short shorts / 13
star chart / 13
late night talk / 13
autumn breeze / 14
wisteria / 14
rhododendron bloom / 14
rereading old love letters / 15
down to the final out / 15
heat lightning / 15

deep inside / 16
broken streetlight / 16
awake / 16
open mic / 17
may moon / 17
dust devil / 17
amid wildflowers / 18
a squirrel / 18
returning to the backyard / 18
estate sale / 19
one white lie / 19
one yawn / 19
late evening / 20
sleepless night / 20
easier said / 20
evening heat / 21
clearing my mind / 21
glazed donut / 21
hanging on / 22
her touch / 22
overnight flight / 22
country road / 23
weenie roast / 23

restless night / 23
all night café / 24
restless night / 24
beaver moon / 24
making the most / 25
eyes closed / 25
after the storm / 25
spacing out— / 26
haze of rain / 26
sinkhole / 26
through the cafe window / 27
foreign trip / 27
twilight / 27
taking / 28
mausoleum garden / 28
late evening / 28
diagnosis day / 29
sultry night / 29
sunday hangover / 29
blood moon / 30
spot light / 30
sibling rivalry / 30
first warm day / 31

talk of cicadas / 31
apple blossom rain / 31
sunrise / 32
finding her pulse / 32
uncorked / 32
morning commute blues / 33
waiting for a sign / 33
city bus / 33
weekday morning / 34
cold front / 34
heat haze / 34
late summer sun / 35
tin ceiling / 35
after the funeral / 35
moonrise / 36
evening breeze / 36
glass emptied / 36
sunday sermon / 37
autumn breeze / 37
farm pond— / 37
lighting a candle / 38
what's left of the orange / 38
shifting embers / 38

super moon / 39

new to our yard / 39

the canoe / 39

harbor bar / 40

autumn's end— / 40

autumn loneliness / 40

morning fog / 41

holding the note / 41

the heat / 41

morning breeze / 42

crosswalk / 42

in and out / 42

far from home / 43

a long line / 43

alone / 43

spring wind / 44

summer stroll / 44

flight delay / 44

unfolding a map / 45

shooting star / 45

dawn / 45

adding cream to the coffee / 46

koi pond / 46

one headlight / 46

midday sun / 47

first day at the beach / 47

afternoon heat / 47

the pub / 48

cigars / 48

a leaf print / 48

morning drizzle / 49

the pause / 49

one star / 49

talking over living wills / 50

one breath / 50

nothing left to say… / 50

*If you want to see something new,
take the same walk every day.*

-Pico Iyer

alone again
at the water's edge...
white egret

shadows lengthening the leap of the grasshopper

agreeing to therapy
dishes dry
on the rack

corner pub
filling the emptiness
of a parking spot

catching the wrong eye across the bar
cocktail bitters

twilight
saying something of the nothing
of it all

spring afternoon
picking the garden
from my fingernails

the itch
of old wool socks
toenail moon

still night...
one jet's journey
across the moon

restless night
the clarity of the riot
in HDTV

blood moon
the suddenness
of the gun

unable to let it go
the word "hope"
on a polished stone

pulling a pen from her hair
the waitress becomes
this poem

fireworks
the burst
of tart lemonade

sultry night
the fiddle holes fill
with sound

poetry reading
the secrets we keep
between paper sheets

backyard weeds everyone has a name

sudden storm—
the quiet place inside
her eyes

dew light
following the web
to the spider

the moth blending into
lichen blending into
stone

midnight
not hearing the silence
until the owl

all day   snow   poems

slowing down the street   evening snow

snow becomes
rain becomes
stars

garden shop
the kid in me finds
the wind chimes

election sermon
the way stained glass
bends the light

empty sky
an old koi
swallows the sun

rising early
to beat the crowd
balloon race

morning drizzle
a little blue boat
still in the sound

deep within the paint
of the old blue guitar
wild horses

twilight
losing sight
of the wiffle ball

spring moon
i, too, am lost
in clouds

moon viewing
i am the oldest
kid

her promise
the still closed buds
of lilac

the heat
of one good lie
harmonica holes

switching tempo
the fiddler deepens
his gaze

short shorts
the curve of
the crescent moon

star chart
all those years through nothing
to be here

late night talk
ice distilling light
in the whisky glass

autumn breeze
finding myself in
grandma's diary

wisteria
the way the breeze teases
her hair

rhododendron bloom
the drone of my own
honey song

rereading old love letters
the shifting shapes
of clouds

down to the final out
the streetlights
switch on

heat lightning
a porch step conversation
with dad

deep inside
dad's old guitar
the cricket

broken streetlight
so much depends upon
the moon

awake
for no other reason
than this poem

open mic
the young poet picks
an old wound

may moon
caught in the gaze
of her tattoo

dust devil
spinning truth
from a lie

amid wildflowers she picks a wedgie

a squirrel
within a squirrel
within a puddle

returning to the backyard
the grackle
of my mind

estate sale
the silence of a clock
from another time

one white lie
becomes two…
riptide

one yawn
now two
jury pool room

late evening
the sudden everywhere
of snow

sleepless night
the opossum passes through
our porch light

easier said
than done
mousetrap

evening heat
blackberries bob
in the bourbon

clearing my mind
indigo bunting

glazed donut
the whole of
my story

hanging on her every word winter moon

her touch
after all these years —
Bach's piano

overnight flight
the shoulder warmth
of a stranger

country road
our headlights pause upon rows
of opossum teeth

weenie roast
the squeezy curves of
condiment bottles

restless night
swiping right through pics
of mars

all night café
the jukebox as strong
as the coffee

restless night
all the words still
in my pen

beaver moon
the smoothness of
shaved skin

making the most
of our silence
winter rain

eyes closed
the old blues man knows
how it goes

after the storm
the mud ruts
of pickup trucks

spacing out—
stars pass across
the skylight

haze of rain
the shapes of men
sandbagging

sinkhole
the question that breaks
everything

through the cafe window
the push and pull
of evening traffic

foreign trip
the many words
for beer

twilight
one by one
dark thoughts appear

taking
the form of corn
summer wind

mausoleum garden
the way the flowers sway
into twilight

late evening
the snow now deeper
than the dog

diagnosis day
coffee rings left
on the counter

sultry night
the tilt of a beer bottle
in the dim bar light

sunday hangover
the hardness
of hail

blood moon
the grip of the vine
on the welcome sign

spot light lifting the flamenco dancer's skirt

sibling rivalry
the aggressiveness of
my brother's fart

first warm day
skirts shorten
the conversation

talk of cicadas
on the porch swing
lavender lemonade

apple blossom rain
last year's sapling big enough
for birdsong

sunrise
cream coloring
the coffee coloring the cream

finding her pulse the piano

uncorked
the night pours
itself

morning commute blues
the backbeat
of potholes

waiting for a sign   crosswalk

city bus
every seat filled
with sun

weekday morning
pulling my mood
off a hanger

cold front
the taste of dark roast coffee
on her tongue

heat haze
the turtle becomes
the silence of a log

late summer sun
darkness at the root of
her ponytail

tin ceiling
grandma talks of a world
before the war

after the funeral
we compare
lifelines

moonrise over the flood wall the river

evening breeze
a dove calls
into it

glass emptied
the evening full
of me

sunday sermon
lengthening—the crack
in the stained glass

autumn breeze
the cadence of colors
across the hill

farm pond —
the way the heron
fills it

lighting a candle
with a candle
another night of snow

what's left of the orange
lingers on my fingers
winter sunset

shifting embers
the glow of everyone
breathing

super moon
tonight it's the whole
truth

new to our yard
we give the cat
a name

the canoe
floating through our silence
summer stars

harbor bar
an ancient mariner rhymes
over whisky

autumn's end —
the silence inside
cicada shells

autumn loneliness
i reach for the last
chicken wing

morning fog
an inchworm dangles
into nothing

holding the note
held by it
fiddle bow

the heat
of her touch
bending spoons

morning breeze
the shimmying shadows
of café umbrellas

crosswalk
the stop and start
of rain

in and out
of the rusted shed
moonshine

far from home
a cafe americano
and johnny cash

a long line
at the confessional
donut sunday

alone
without a pen
the language of birds

spring wind
spinning the barstool
the kid in me

summer stroll
syncing our steps
to sprinklers

flight delay
the familiar faces
of strangers

unfolding a map
the ocean
between us

shooting star
i reshuffle
the tarot

dawn
the cold of porcelain
before coffee

adding cream to the coffee
she makes her point
again

koi pond
the open mouths
of children

one headlight
crossing the river
the moon

midday sun
the fence's shadow
switching yards

first day at the beach
i struggle to read between
the tan lines

afternoon heat
we immigrate into
a watermelon

the pub
full of old friends
that aren't mine

cigars
lighting up
a conversation

a leaf print
in the latte
the barista's tattoo

morning drizzle
the way they sway in the pine
bagworms

the pause
before the light turns green
i become a deer

one star
now two...
frog songs

talking over living wills
the hum of appliances

one breath
then another
tingsha bells

nothing left to say…
the oak's
bare branches

Ben Gaa is "your friendly neighborhood haiku poet" from St. Louis, Missouri. He is a Pushcart nominee and the author of the 2018 Touchstone Award winning *Wishbones* (Folded Word 2018), a full length collection of haiku and senryu, as well as three haiku/senryu chapbooks, *Fiddle in the Floorboards* (Yavanika Press 2018), *Blowing on a Hot Soup Spoon* (poor metaphor 2014) and the Pushcart nominated *Wasp Shadows* (Folded Word 2014). His poems have appeared in numerous journals and anthologies around the globe. He has a degree in Creative Writing from Knox College, works as a Senior IT Functional Analyst for MilliporeSigma, and enjoys travel, music, art and other worldly meanderings. Find out more about Ben at www.benmoellergaa.com.

www.ingramcontent.com/pod-product-compliance
Lightning Source LLC
Chambersburg PA
CBHW030137100526
44592CB00011B/933